S0-ALL-621

PICTURE WINDOW BOOKS
World Atlases

ATLAS of the

Poles and Oceans

by Karen Foster

PICTURE WINDOW BOOKS

Minneapolis, Minnesota

First American edition published in 2008 by
Picture Window Books
151 Good Counsel Drive
P.O. Box 669
Mankato, MN 56002-0669
877-845-8392
www.picturewindowbooks.com

Editors: Jill Kalz and Shelly Lyons
Designer: Hilary Wacholz
Page Production: Ashlee Schultz
Art Director: Nathan Gassman
Associate Managing Editor: Christianne Jones
Content Adviser: Lisa Thornquist, Ph.D., Geography
Cartographer: XNR Productions, Inc. (9, 11, 13, 20-21)

Editor and Compiler: Karen Foster
Factual Researcher: Joe Josephs
Designers: Fanny Masters & Maia Terry
Picture Researcher: Diana Morris
Illustrators: Rebecca Elliott, Ali Lodge, and Q2 Media
Maps: Geo-Innovations UK

Printed in the United States of America.

Foster, Karen.
Atlas of the Poles and Oceans / by Karen Foster. - Minneapolis, MN : Picture Window Books, 2008.
32 p. : col. ill., col. maps ; cm. - (Picture Window Books world atlases).
2-4
2-4.
Includes index and glossary.
ISBN 978-1-4048-3886-4 (library binding)
ISBN 978-1-4048-3894-9 (paperback)
1. Maps-Juvenile literature. 2. North Pole-Geography-Juvenile literature. 3. South Pole-Geography-Juvenile literature. 4. North Pole-Maps for children. 5. South Pole-Maps for children.
G863   919.98 REF
                                                DLC

Photo Credits:
Age Fotostock/Superstock: 6bl. Kapor Baldev/Corbis: 25b. Peter Batson/Imagequestmarine.com: 24t. Morton Beebe/Corbis: 26t. Yann Arthus-Bertrand/Corbis: 22. Vera Bogaerts Shutterstock: 15br. Sandy Buckley/iStockphoto: 27t. Tim Davis/Corbis: 26b. Natalie Forbes/Corbis: 27bl. Stephen Frink/Corbis: 23tr. Beat Glanzman/zefa/Corbis: 14br. Jeff Goldman/Shutterstock: 6tr. Chris Howey/Shutterstock: 8br. Peter Johnson/Corbis: 6br. Bob Krist/Corbis: 28-29. Kurt/Dreamstime: compass rose on 4, 16, 20, 22, 24; Nik Nikiz/Shutterstock: 8b, 15tr. Pat O'Hara/Corbis: 15bl. Jeffrey L. Rotman/Corbis: 23br. Galen Rowell/Corbis: 14t. Anders Ryman/Corbis: 15tl. Ricky Subiantoputra/Shutterstock: 25t. Stuart Westmorland/Corbis: 23bl. Nik Wheeler/Corbis: 14bl. Ralph White/Corbis: 24b.

Editor's Note: The maps in this book were created with the Miller projection.

Table of Contents

Welcome to the Poles and Oceans. 4

Antarctica. 6

The Arctic. 8

Plants of Antarctica and the Arctic . . . 10

Animals of Antarctica and the Arctic . . . 12

People of the Polar Regions. 14

The Five Oceans 16

The Ocean Floor 18

Ocean Climate 20

Atlantic Ocean 22

Pacific Ocean. 24

Indian Ocean 25

Protecting the Environment 26

Journey to the North Pole 28

Poles and Oceans At-a-Glance 30

Glossary. 31

Index 32

Welcome to the Poles and Oceans

The world is made up of five oceans and seven chunks of land called continents: North America, South America, Antarctica, Europe, Africa, Asia, and Australia. This map shows Antarctica's position in the world.

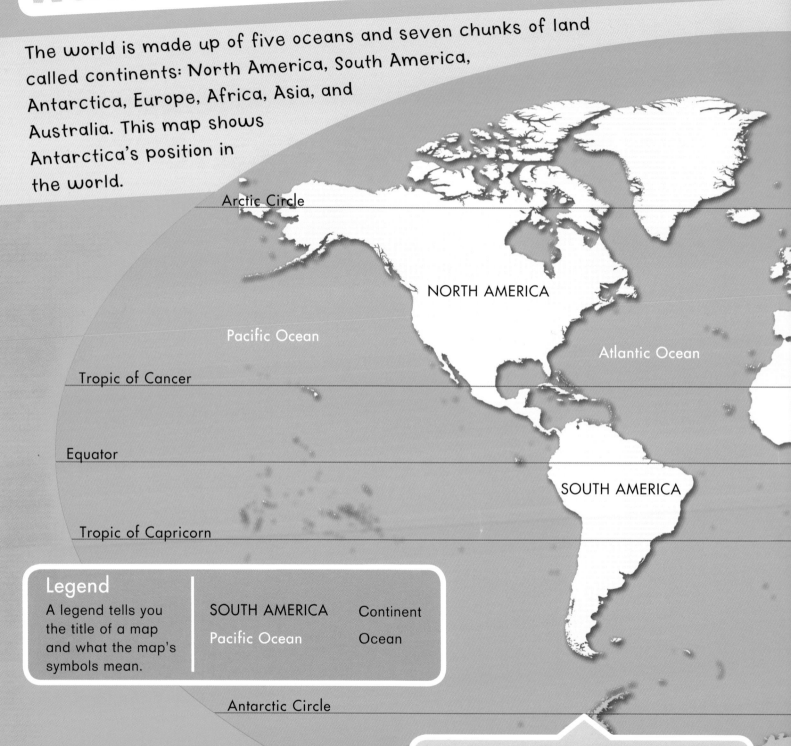

Arctic Circle

NORTH AMERICA

Pacific Ocean

Atlantic Ocean

Tropic of Cancer

Equator

SOUTH AMERICA

Tropic of Capricorn

Legend
A legend tells you the title of a map and what the map's symbols mean.

SOUTH AMERICA	Continent
Pacific Ocean	Ocean

Antarctic Circle

The Antarctic Circle is an imaginary line in the southern part of the world that marks the edge of the Antarctic region.

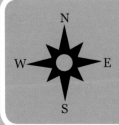

Compass Rose
A compass rose shows you the four cardinal directions: north (N), south (S), east (E), and west (W).

The South Pole lies in Antarctica. The North Pole lies in the Arctic region. Between the poles lie five oceans: the Pacific Ocean, the Atlantic Ocean, the Indian Ocean, the Arctic Ocean, and the Southern Ocean. The oceans make up three-fourths of Earth's surface.

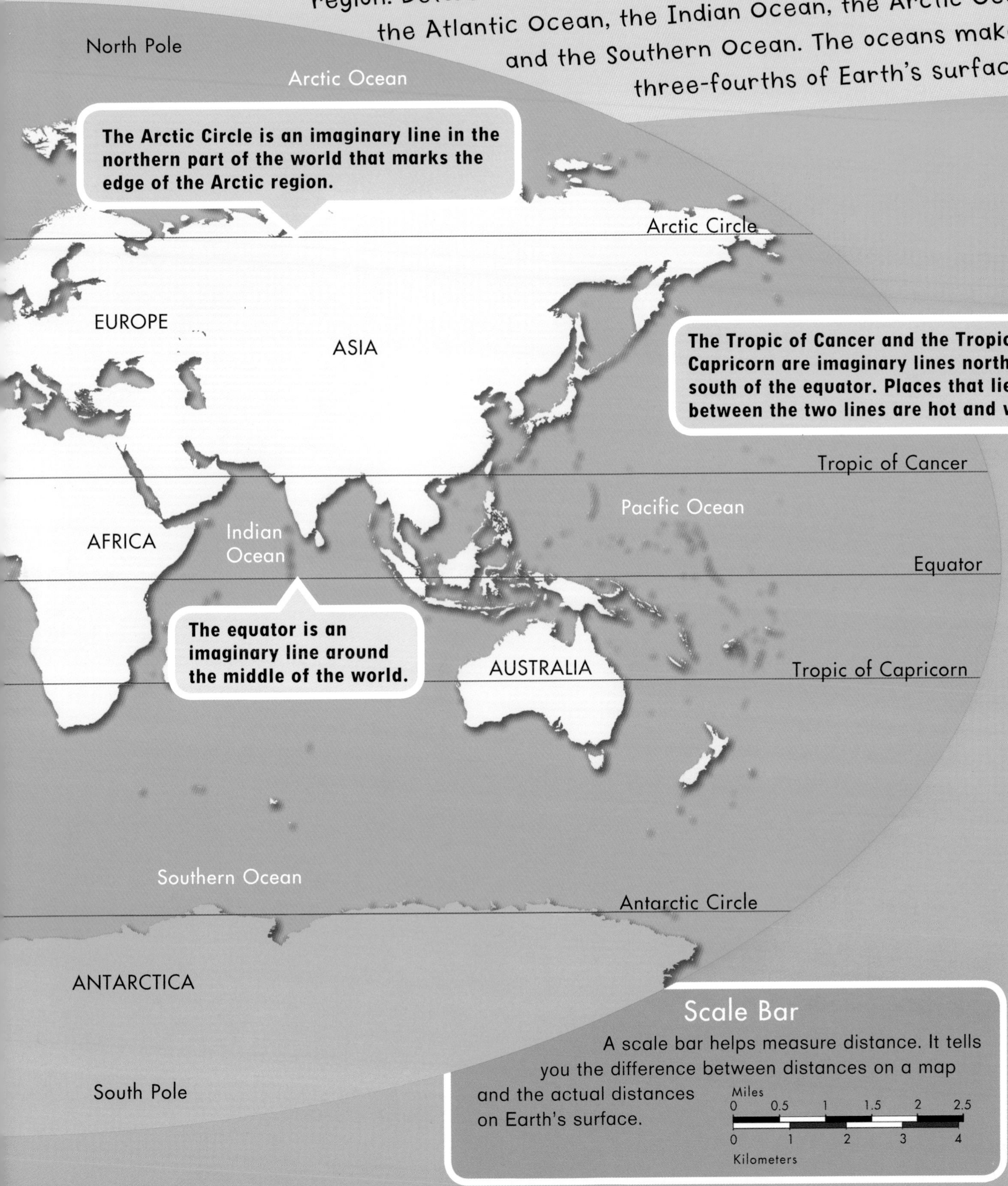

North Pole

Arctic Ocean

The Arctic Circle is an imaginary line in the northern part of the world that marks the edge of the Arctic region.

Arctic Circle

EUROPE

ASIA

The Tropic of Cancer and the Tropic of Capricorn are imaginary lines north and south of the equator. Places that lie between the two lines are hot and wet.

Tropic of Cancer

Pacific Ocean

AFRICA

Indian Ocean

Equator

The equator is an imaginary line around the middle of the world.

AUSTRALIA

Tropic of Capricorn

Southern Ocean

Antarctic Circle

ANTARCTICA

Scale Bar

A scale bar helps measure distance. It tells you the difference between distances on a map and the actual distances on Earth's surface.

South Pole

Miles
0   0.5   1   1.5   2   2.5

0   1   2   3   4
Kilometers

Antarctica

Antarctica is the fifth-largest of Earth's seven continents. It lies in the most southern region of the world. It is surrounded by the Southern Ocean.

Except for a few dry valleys in the mountains, Antarctica is covered by a huge sheet of snow and ice. In some places, the ice is nearly 2 miles (3.2 kilometers) thick.

Antarctica is the coldest, windiest place on Earth. Because the continent gets very little precipitation, it is also known as the world's largest cold desert.

The highest mountain

Vinson Massif is the highest mountain in Antarctica. Instead of having one tall peak, it has many. The tallest is 16,067 feet (4,900 meters). Because of its height and location, Vinson Massif is very cold. The average summer temperature is about minus 20 degrees Fahrenheit (minus 29 degrees Celsius).

One of Vinson Massif's snow-covered peaks

A giant ice shelf

The Ross Ice Shelf is the largest ice shelf in Antarctica. It's about the size of France! In 2000, a huge chunk broke off and fell into the sea. It was 170 miles (272 km) long and 25 miles (40 km) wide!

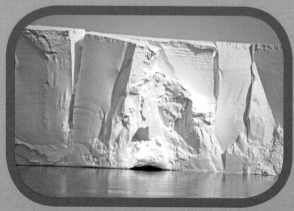

The edge of the Ross Ice Shelf

The Southern Ocean

The Southern Ocean is the second-smallest ocean in the world. It surrounds Antarctica and borders no other continents. Its surface area is 7.8 million square miles (20.3 million square kilometers). The Southern Ocean is believed to be Earth's youngest ocean, at about 30 million years old.

There are billions of tiny creatures called krill in the Southern Ocean.

Major Landforms

● place of interest ----- ice shelf boundary ☐ ice cap 🏔 mountain ⬜ ice shelf

Antarctic Circle

Southern Ocean

Queen Maud Land

Enderby Land

Antarctic Peninsula

Weddell Sea

Ronne Ice Shelf

ANTARCTICA

Amery Ice Shelf

Bellinghausen Sea

American Highland

Transantarctic Mountains

Ellsworth Land

Vinson Massif

● South Pole

Amundsen Sea

Marie Byrd Land

Ross Ice Shelf

McMurdo Station

Ross Sea

Mount Erebus

Wilkes Land

- About 90 percent of the world's ice lies in Antarctica.
- In the center of the continent, the average monthly temperature is between minus 20 and minus 60 degrees Fahrenheit (minus 29 and minus 51 degrees Celsius).
- From the South Pole, all directions are north.
- Mount Erebus is a volcano that rises from the Ross Sea. Despite the cold climate, a large lake of melted rock (lava) boils inside the volcano.

7

The Arctic

The Arctic is a large area of water, ice, and frozen land that surrounds the North Pole. It is often defined as the region within the Arctic Circle.

During the Arctic's short summer, the ice sheet shrinks. But in winter, when the temperature drops, the ice sheet grows again.

Several countries lie partly in the Arctic. These include Canada, Finland, Norway, Sweden, Russia, and the United States. Most of the island of Greenland also lies in the Arctic.

Land of the Midnight Sun

The area north of the Arctic Circle is often called the Land of the Midnight Sun. The sun shines 24 hours a day there in late June and early July. In December and January, however, the sky is dark nearly all day, and temperatures drop very low.

A time-lapse photo of the midnight sun over northern Sweden in the summer

Ice caves

Inside the glaciers of Greenland are mazes of ice caves. During the summer, the glaciers' surface ice begins to melt. Water rushes down the slopes and runs into deep cracks. It carves tunnels and caves in the glaciers.

The tunnels inside Greenland's glaciers glow blue.

The Arctic Ocean

The world's northern-most ocean, the Arctic Ocean, is the smallest of Earth's five oceans. Its surface area is 5.4 million square miles (14 million square kilometers). That's about one and a half times the size of the United States. The Arctic Ocean touches the continents of North America, Europe, and Asia.

The cold waters of the Arctic Ocean

Major Landforms

- ● place of interest
- ----- ice shelf boundary
- —— country boundary
- ▨ pack ice
- 🔺 mountain
- 🛑 plateau
- ▨ ice shelf

Arctic Circle

Brooks
Mountains

Anadyr
Mountains

UNITED
STATES

East
Siberian
Sea

Verkhoyansk
Mountains

NORTH
AMERICA

Beaufort Sea

CANADA

RUSSIA

Laptev Sea

ASIA

Arctic Ocean

Putorana
Plateau

● North Pole

Ellesmere
Island

Ward Hunt
Ice Shelf

Arctic
Rockies

Baffin
Island

Kara
Sea

Baffin Bay

Ural
Mountains

GREENLAND
(DENMARK)

Barents Sea

Kjolen
Mountains

EUROPE

FINLAND

NORWAY

SWEDEN

- • From the North Pole, all directions are south.
- • Pack ice is floating frozen ocean water. It forms, grows, and melts in the ocean.
- • Much of the land inside the Arctic Circle has huge glaciers that flow to the coasts. These glaciers have carved out valleys, peaks, and steep hills.
- • The largest ice shelf in the Arctic is the Ward Hunt Ice Shelf. It lies on Canada's Ellesmere Island and is 3,000 years old.

9

Plants of Antarctica and the Arctic

Few plants can grow in Antarctica. Those that do are small and grow close to the coasts. Much of the continent's ground is hard and cold, making it difficult for plants to grow long roots.

The many hundreds of plants in the Arctic region are well-adapted to the forest and tundra ecosystems. An ecosystem is all of the living and nonliving things in a certain area. It includes plants, animals, soil, weather ... everything!

Some Plants of Antarctica

ice cap

lichen

Lichen is a mosslike plant that grows mostly on the rocky coasts of Antarctica. But it has been found on rocks close to the South Pole, too.

moss

Mosses are some of the oldest plants in Antarctica. They grow in wet, low-lying areas along the coasts.

Some Plants of the Arctic

forest

pine tree

Pine trees are a type of evergreen tree called a conifer. They have needlelike leaves and produce cones.

cranberry

Cranberry creeps over the floor of the northern forests. It has pink flowers and small red berries.

arctic poppy

Yellow and white poppies grow in Arctic forests and meadows. They turn their heads toward the sun.

tundra

cotton grass

Cotton grass grows in wet areas of the tundra. It has a white, feathery flower that breaks apart and blows away with the wind.

liverwort

Liverwort is a small, low-growing plant. It attaches itself to the ground or to rocks with thin threads instead of roots.

dwarf willow

The dwarf willow is the smallest tree in the world. It grows only 4 inches (10 centimeters) tall.

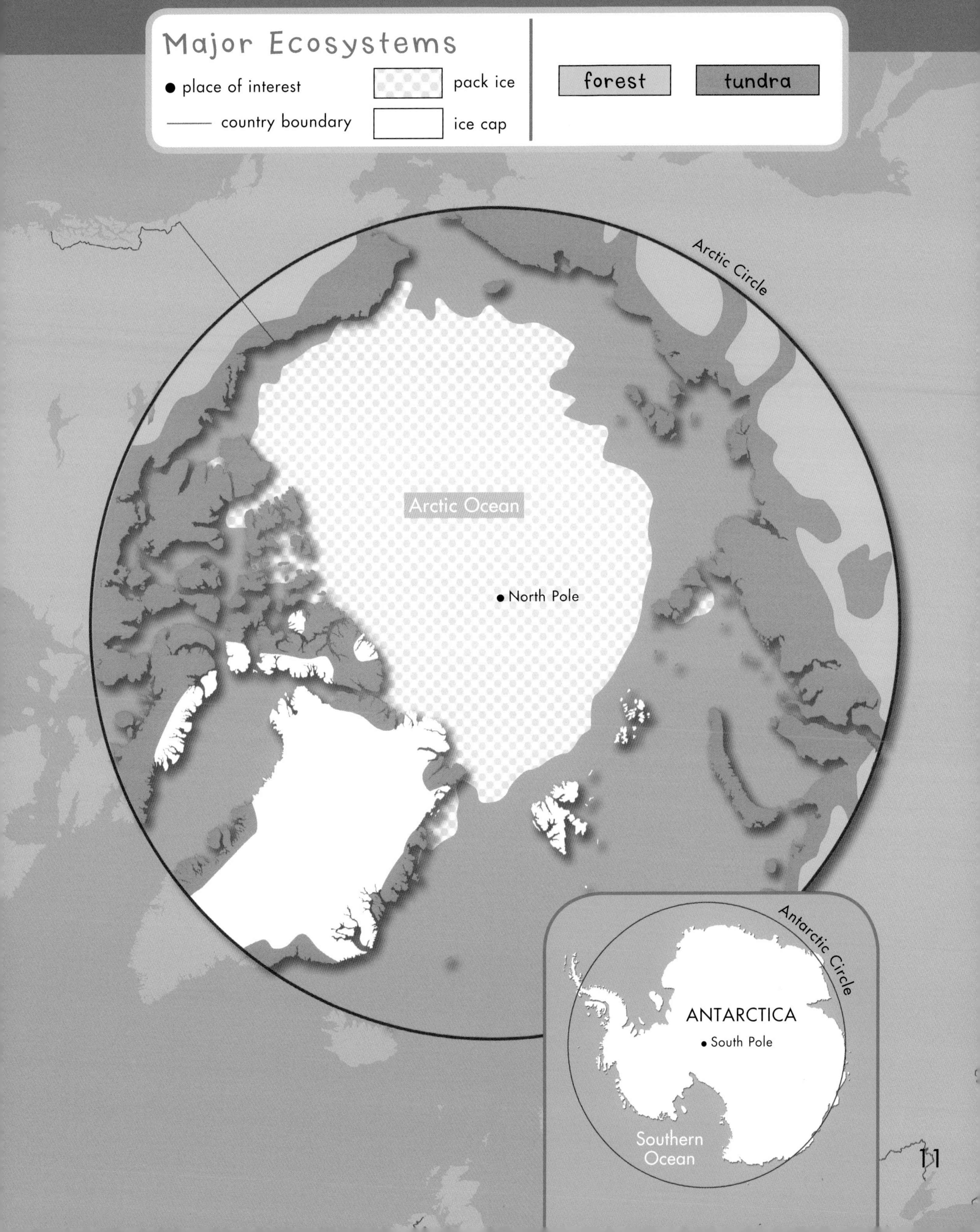

Major Ecosystems

- ● place of interest
- —— country boundary
- ▦ pack ice
- ☐ ice cap
- forest
- tundra

Arctic Circle

Arctic Ocean

● North Pole

Antarctic Circle

ANTARCTICA

● South Pole

Southern
Ocean

Animals of Antarctica and the Arctic

It is too cold for animals to live in central Antarctica. But around the continent's warmer coasts are plenty of penguins and other birds, fish, and seals.

Polar bears live on pack ice in the Arctic. But most other Arctic animals live in the region's tundra and forest ecosystems. An ecosystem is all of the living and nonliving things in a certain area.

Some Animals of Antarctica

ice cap

	emperor penguin	Male emperor penguins warm their mates' eggs on their feet throughout the bitterly cold Antarctic winter.
	icefish	Icefish live in Antarctic waters. Their bodies make a special liquid that stops their blood from freezing.

	petrel	The petrel is white with black eyes. It nests on icebergs off Antarctica's rocky shores.
	elephant seal	Elephant seals are huge and have large, floppy noses. Male elephant seals are fierce fighters.

Some Animals of the Arctic

forest

	ermine	The ermine's body is long and slender. It can easily chase mice and other prey through narrow underground tunnels.
	wolverine	The wolverine has big, furry feet that act like snowshoes. They keep the animal from sinking into the snow.
	brown bear	The brown bear lives in the forests of Russia. It feeds on roots, nuts, berries, fish, and small animals.

pack ice

	polar bear	Polar bears prowl the ice in the Arctic. They build snow caves to shelter their young.

tundra

	reindeer	Reindeer move across the Arctic in herds. Some herds may include thousands of reindeer.
	arctic hare	In the winter, the arctic hare's fur turns white. It sits so still on the snow that it is almost invisible to other animals.
	musk ox	The musk ox has a thick overcoat of long, shaggy hair that hangs down to the ground.

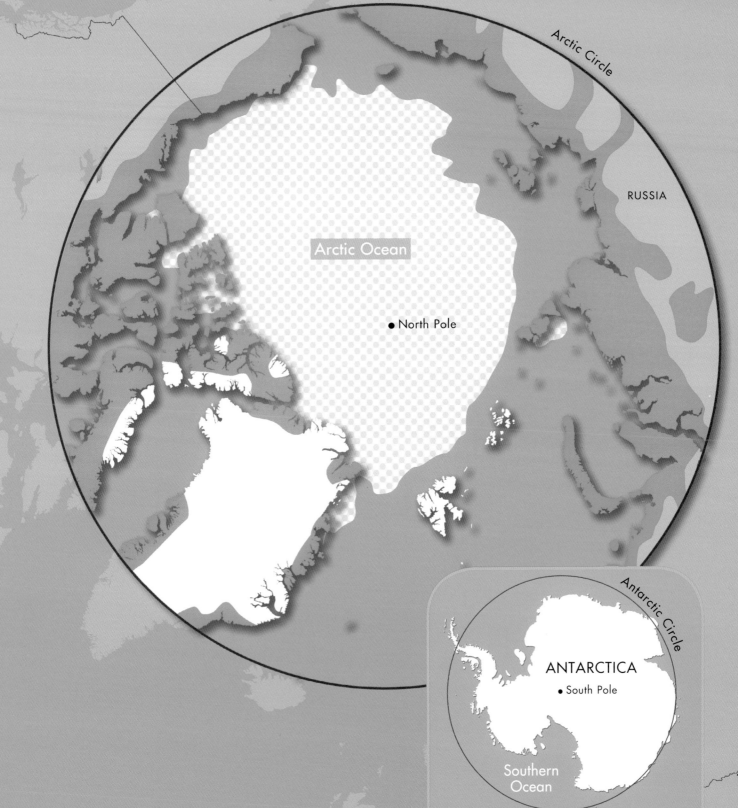

Major Ecosystems

- ● place of interest
- —— country boundary
- pack ice
- ice cap
- forest
- tundra

Arctic Circle

RUSSIA

Arctic Ocean

● North Pole

Antarctic Circle

ANTARCTICA
● South Pole

Southern Ocean

People of the Polar Regions

The only people who live in Antarctica are teams of scientists. They are there only part of the year. They live and work in research stations along the coasts.

The Arctic, on the other hand, is home to many groups of people, including the Chukchi, Inuit, and Sami. They have adapted their clothing, homes, transportation, and ways of finding food to the Arctic's harsh climate.

The Inuit

The Inuit people live in Canada and Greenland. They protect themselves from the cold with clothing made from the skins of Arctic animals such as reindeer, seals, polar bears, and even birds.

The Inuit stay warm in the Arctic cold by wearing animal skin boots and fur-lined parkas and mittens.

The Sami

The Sami, or Lapps, live in Norway, Sweden, and Finland. They used to move from place to place, fishing, trapping animals for fur, and herding sheep and reindeer. Today, most Sami lead modern lives in the cities and have modern jobs.

A Sami child wears bright, colorful wool clothes with thick shoes to stay warm.

The Chukchi

The Chukchi live in Arctic Russia. They used to hunt walruses and whales from kayaks (canoe-like boats) using spears. Today they use guns and travel in motorboats and on snowmobiles.

In the winter, Inuit hunters use blocks of snow to build overnight shelters called igloos.

Arctic transportation

People cross the Arctic landscape in various ways. They ride snowmobiles or dogsleds. They cross-country ski. They walk with snowshoes so their feet won't sink into the snow.

A Sami family gets ready for a snowmobile ride.

Earning a living

Today, many Inuit in Canada earn their living in the mining and building industries. They also work in the tourism industry, taking visitors on dogsled and hunting trips. Some Inuit sell traditional hand-carved art to tourists.

A piece of carved Inuit art

Polar explorers

The Norwegian explorer Roald Amundsen was the first person to reach the South Pole, in 1912. He used skis and a dogsled to get there. The British explorer Robert Scott came second. He was the first to drag his own sled across Antarctica.

Until about 100 years ago, no person had explored Antarctica.

Antarctic research stations

Scientists from many countries have set up research stations in Antarctica to study the ice, rocks, animals, and climate. Most scientists leave the continent before winter sets in. McMurdo Station is home to about 1,000 people and is Antarctica's most-populated community.

Antarctic research stations must be able to withstand bitter cold and very strong winds.

The Five Oceans

About 97 percent of all water in the world is in Earth's five oceans: the Pacific Ocean, the Atlantic Ocean, the Indian Ocean, the Arctic Ocean, and the Southern Ocean. The largest of the oceans is the Pacific Ocean.

The average depth of the oceans is 12,460 feet (3,800 meters) or about 10 Empire State Buildings stacked on top of each other.

Each ocean has layers, or zones. Each zone has its own animals and plants. There are more than 1 million known species of ocean plants and animals.

Salty water

The oceans have always been salty. Long ago, rain poured onto Earth for millions of years. The rainwater formed rivers that flowed to low areas of land. The rainwater pooled there and formed oceans. When the rainwater ran over rocks, it took in salt, and that made the ocean water salty.

High and low tides

The moon and sun pull on Earth. The moon's pull causes the surface of an ocean to rise. Ocean water swells toward the moon when the moon is closest to it. This causes a high tide. The ocean water falls when the moon is farther away. This causes a low tide. During high tide, the pulling motion causes the water on the opposite side of the planet to also swell. The Earth spins around once in a day, so an ocean has two high tides in one day.

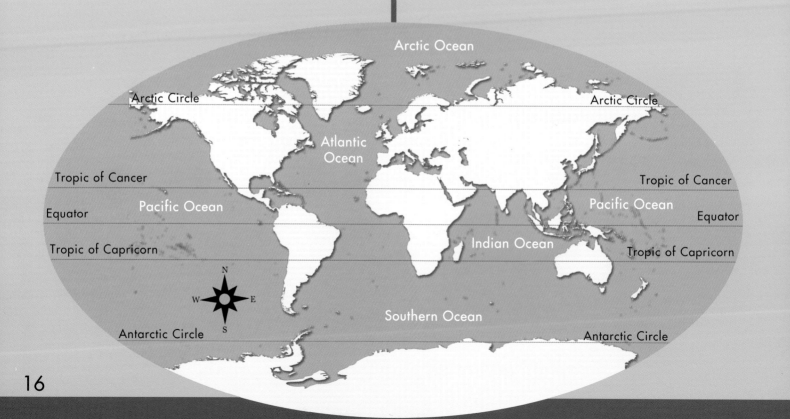

Some Plants and Animals of the Oceans

sea level

dolphin	Dolphins are warm-blooded animals and use lungs to breathe. They are one of the few mammals that spend their entire lives in water.	
plankton	Plankton are tiny plants and animals that live near the surface of the ocean. They float through the water together in large masses.	sunlit zone
tuna	Tuna are one of the fastest fish in the world, reaching speeds of up to 45 miles (72 kilometers) per hour.	
blue whale	With a length of up to 100 feet (31 m) and a weight of more than 150 tons (135 metric tons), the blue whale is believed to be the largest animal on Earth.	twilight zone
jellyfish	Jellyfish have no bones and look like floating bags of water. Some of them glow.	
viper fish	The viper fish lives deep in the ocean during the day. But at night, it moves to shallower water to eat. It has a giant mouth and long, sharp teeth.	midnight zone
gulper eel	The gulper eel has a long, thin body that helps it hide easily from other animals. Its dark coloring also helps it hide in the dark midnight zone.	
kelp	Kelp is a type of seaweed that grows in cold ocean water. It is brown or green and can grow to be 100 feet (31 m) long.	ocean floor

The Ocean Floor

The land under Earth's oceans is not flat and sandy. In fact, it's very much like the dry land of the continents. It's made up of tall mountains, deep valleys, and wide, flat plains.

The ocean floor is an amazing place. The tallest landform and lowest point on Earth are found in the ocean.

The world's tallest mountain is Mount Kea in Hawaii. From the base at the bottom of the Pacific Ocean to its peak high in the sky, this mountain measures 33,476 feet (10,210 meters). While Mount Everest and other peaks are higher above sea level, Mount Kea is the tallest from bottom to top.

The world's lowest point is the Mariana Trench, which lies in the Pacific Ocean. At 35,840 feet (10,931 m) deep, it is deeper than Mount Everest—the highest mountain on land—is tall.

Continental shelf

A continental shelf is the flat, underwater edge of a continent. These shelves can be from 50 miles (80 kilometers) wide to 900 miles (1,440 km) wide. Continental shelves make up about 50 percent of the Arctic Ocean floor. No other ocean floor has as many continental shelves.

Continental slope

The outer part of the continental shelf begins to slope before it makes a steep drop to the ocean floor. The steep drop is called the continental slope, which is the true edge of a continent.

Abyssal plain

The smooth, nearly flat area of the ocean floor is called the abyssal plain. It starts at the bottom of the continental slope. This is truly the bottom of the ocean.

Underwater volcanoes

The oceans even have volcanoes! The Mariana Arc is a chain of underwater volcanoes in the Pacific Ocean. A volcano is a type of mountain that can throw hot, melted rock (lava), ashes, and gases from deep inside Earth. Volcanoes can erupt at ocean ridges and trenches. When they erupt above sea level, they form volcanic islands.

- Most islands began as volcanoes. The Hawaiian Islands formed when volcanoes erupted under the Pacific Ocean.
- More than half of the volcanoes in the world are found underwater and on land around the rim of the Pacific Ocean. This circle is called the Ring of Fire.
- There are mountains in every ocean. If placed together, they would form a chain more than 37,300 miles (59,680 km) long.

Mid-ocean ridge

The mid-ocean ridge is a mountain chain with the most active volcanic area on Earth. Deep in the ocean, it winds its way around the continents. It's four times as long as the continents' major mountain ranges (the Andes, the Rocky Mountains, and the Himalayas) combined.

Seamount

A seamount is an underwater mountain with a height of at least 3,300 feet (1,000 m). Most seamounts are volcanoes with peaks that do not reach the surface of the ocean. More than 50 percent of all seamounts are in the Pacific Ocean.

Sea trench

Sea trenches are large valleys in the ocean floor. They are formed when two moving sections of Earth's floor meet, and one slides beneath the other. Because of this movement, deep-sea trenches are the most active part of the deep ocean.

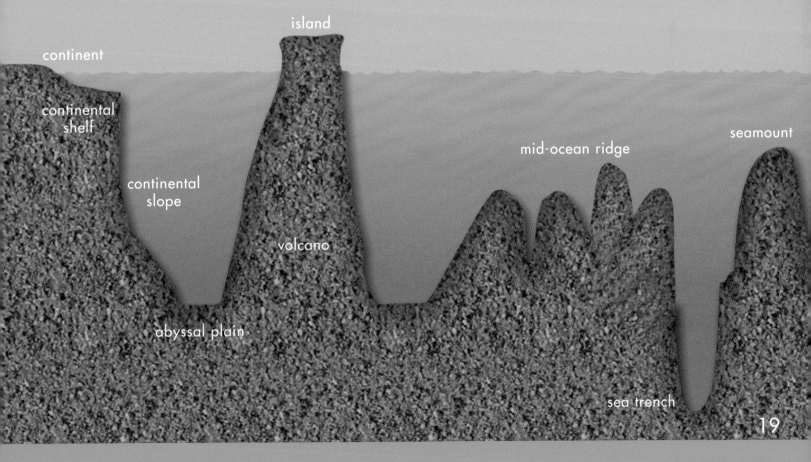

continent

island

continental shelf

continental slope

mid-ocean ridge

seamount

volcano

abyssal plain

sea trench

Ocean Climate

Oceans affect the world's weather and climate. Warm currents, or streams of ocean water, bring a mild climate to the nearby land. Cold currents bring a cool climate.

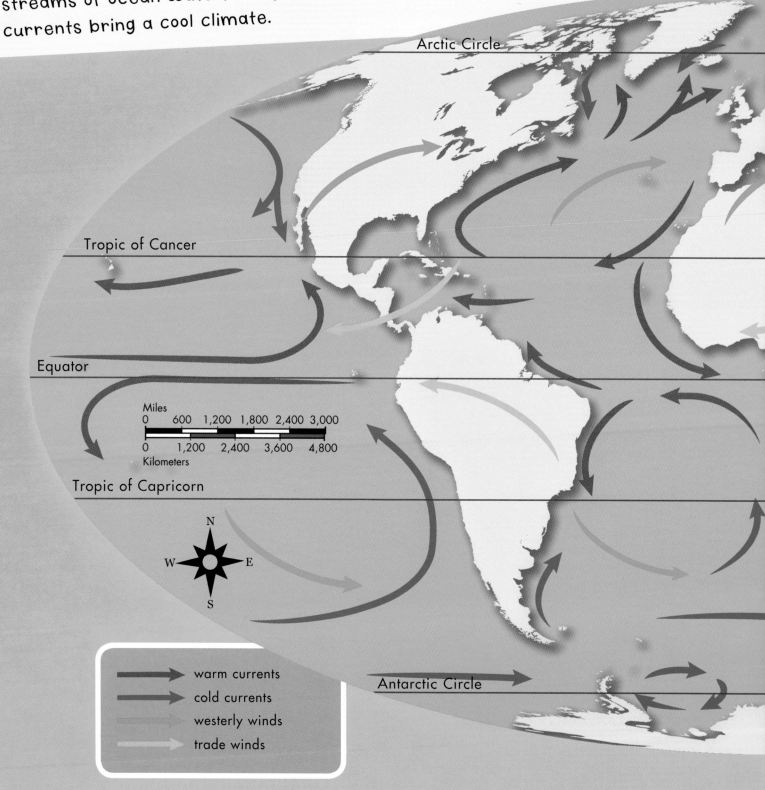

Arctic Circle

Tropic of Cancer

Equator

Miles
0   600   1,200   1,800   2,400   3,000

0   1,200   2,400   3,600   4,800
Kilometers

Tropic of Capricorn

N
W   E
S

Antarctic Circle

warm currents
cold currents
westerly winds
trade winds

Winds also affect the world's weather and climate. They blow from various directions, bringing anything from cool breezes to hot and steamy air masses. Westerly winds blow from the west to the east. Trade winds blow almost constantly in one direction, usually toward the equator from the east.

Arctic Circle

Tropic of Cancer

Equator

Tropic of Capricorn

Antarctic Circle

• Currents can work with or against the ships that bring food and goods from faraway lands.

• Near the equator is an area called the doldrums. This is where little or no wind blows. The sea is calm. Sailboats can be stuck here for days or weeks before the wind picks up again.

• Strong windstorms over the oceans are called hurricanes.

Atlantic Ocean

The Atlantic Ocean is the world's second-largest ocean. It borders the continents of North America and South America on the west and Europe and Africa on the east. It also touches both the Arctic Ocean and the Southern Ocean.

The Atlantic Ocean's total area is about 34 million square miles (88.4 million square kilometers). Its deepest point lies 28,232 feet (8,611 meters) below the surface.

Mid-Atlantic Ridge

The floor of the Atlantic Ocean is divided by the Mid-Atlantic Ridge, a chain of underwater mountains. It is part of the mid-ocean ridge system that snakes across three oceans. Some parts of the Mid-Atlantic Ridge are 500 miles (800 km) wide. In places, the mountains rise above the sea as islands.

An underwater volcano in the Mid-Atlantic Ridge erupted and formed an island.

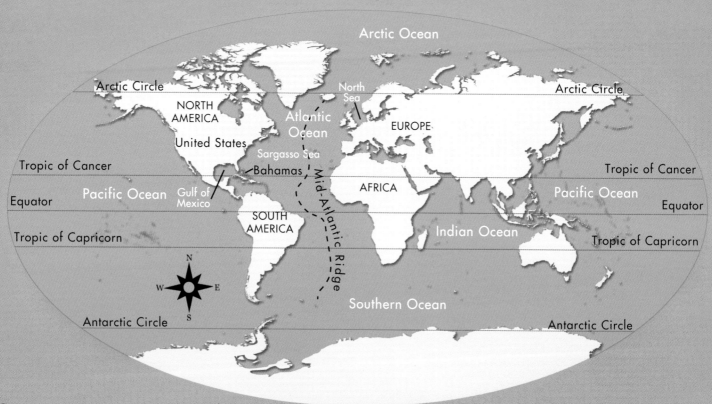

Arctic Ocean

Arctic Circle

North Sea

Arctic Circle

NORTH AMERICA

Atlantic Ocean

EUROPE

United States

Sargasso Sea

Tropic of Cancer

Bahamas

AFRICA

Tropic of Cancer

Pacific Ocean

Gulf of Mexico

Mid-Atlantic Ridge

Pacific Ocean

Equator

Equator

SOUTH AMERICA

Tropic of Capricorn

Indian Ocean

Tropic of Capricorn

N

W   E

S

Southern Ocean

Antarctic Circle

Antarctic Circle

Sea grass meadows

Sea grass grows in the shallow, sunlit waters southeast of the United States. These underwater grass meadows are home to small animals. Baby seahorses hold onto blades of grass, and lobsters feed there before moving into deeper water.

Blue holes

The Bahamas is a chain of islands in the Atlantic Ocean that are southeast of the United States. The islands lie on soft rock banks. Long ago, these banks rose above sea level. Rainwater wore away the rock, making caves and canyons. Today, the holes are flooded with seawater and are called blue holes. Strange cave creatures called troglobites live here. Because the pools are so dark, their skin is very pale. Many of them are blind or have no eyes at all.

There are more than 50 blue holes in the shallow water off the Bahamas.

Reef walls

The coast of Grand Bahama Island in the Bahamas is circled by a coral reef. The steep walls of the reef have caves. Sponges and sea fans, types of ocean animals, stick out from the walls.

Reef walls near the Bahamas

Seaweed jungles

In the clear, warm, and salty Sargasso Sea, in the middle of the North Atlantic, there are floating seaweed jungles. The seaweed has been pushed there by ocean currents. The Sargasso Sea is a breeding ground for eels and a home for loggerhead sea turtles that hatch off the North American coast.

Seaweed jungle, Sargasso Sea

- In the North Sea and Gulf of Mexico, huge amounts of oil and natural gas are trapped under the rocks of the ocean floor. The oil and gas were formed from the mineral remains of dead sea creatures.
- The Atlantic Ocean makes up 17 percent of Earth's total surface area.

23

Pacific Ocean

The Pacific Ocean is the largest of the five oceans. In fact, it covers almost one-third of Earth's surface.

The Pacific Ocean's borders touch many countries. Its southern border touches the Southern Ocean. Its northern border is the Bering Sea.

The deepest place on Earth is found in the Pacific Ocean. It reaches 35,840 feet (10,931 meters) below the surface of the water.

Strong storms and volcanic eruptions take place in Pacific Ocean waters.

Worm city

Giant red worms live inside white tubes attached to huge hot-water vents on the ocean floor. The worms feed on the minerals inside the vents. The vents also support many animals such as clams, mussels, and shrimps.

Giant tube worms live in vents on the ocean floor.

Black smokers

At the bottom of the Pacific Ocean, hot water full of minerals pours from towering tunnels. The water is warmed by hot rocks inside vents, or cracks, in the ocean floor. The minerals harden around the vents as the hot water cools. As more minerals are laid down, the tunnels grow taller and taller. They are called black smokers because dark-colored minerals from the vents turn the water black.

A black smoker

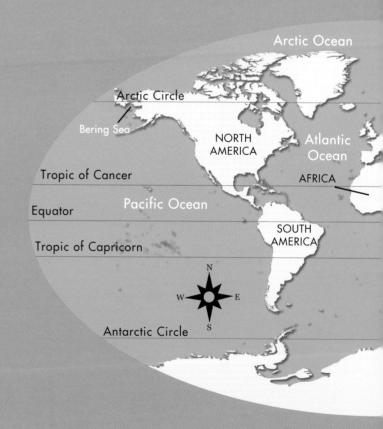

Arctic Ocean

Arctic Circle

Bering Sea

NORTH AMERICA

Atlantic Ocean

Tropic of Cancer

AFRICA

Equator

Pacific Ocean

SOUTH AMERICA

Tropic of Capricorn

Antarctic Circle

Indian Ocean

The third-largest ocean in the world is the Indian Ocean. It touches Australia on the east and Africa on the west. Asia is to the north, and the Southern Ocean is to the south.

The total surface area of the Indian Ocean is 26.6 million square miles (69.2 million square kilometers).

Important sea routes in the Indian Ocean connect Africa and Asia with Europe, North America, and South America.

The Sunda Arc

The islands of Sumatra and Java in the Indian Ocean form the spine of the Sunda Arc. The Sundra Arc is a chain of volcanoes that are regularly shaken by earthquakes and tidal waves. A volcano is a kind of mountain that can throw hot, melted rock (lava), ashes, and gases from deep inside Earth.

Smoke rises from Mount Bromo, Java.

Bay of Bengal

In the northeastern Indian Ocean is the Bay of Bengal. Tropical storms move from the ocean to land. Sometimes the storms cause the rivers in the area to flood.

Flooding of the Ganges River near the Bay of Bengal

Protecting the Environment

Experts agree that global warming is quickly changing the planet. The seas are getting warmer. Near the poles, this warmer water causes the ice caps to gradually melt. It also causes glaciers to flow into the oceans much faster than before. Rising sea water and melting ice take away the homes and food sources of many animals.

Scientists say global warming is caused by pollution from humans. Pollution is made up of harmful materials and wastes. Fishing, hunting, oil spills, and other human activities also harm oceans and polar areas. But many people are working to protect the poles and oceans.

Stories in the ice

Scientists dig down into the ice to find traces of the past. Each layer of ice represents a single year of snowfall, including everything that fell into the snow—dust, ash, gases, and more. Ice cores taken from under the surface of Greenland's ice show that the air has been polluted with lead from gasoline for many years.

Scientists collect ice cores by driving a hollow tube deep into the thick ice sheets of Antarctica, Greenland, and other polar areas.

A polar bear jumps from one chunk of ice to another.

Bears on ice

Global warming is a threat to polar bears. The bears depend on an icy platform to hunt for seals. But as the ice melts, they have to swim farther and farther away to catch their prey. Warmer weather shortens the bears' hunting season, which can cause bears to starve.

Antarctica: the last wilderness

In 1959, more than 40 countries agreed to the Antarctic Treaty. This protects the continent because it only allows peaceful and scientific use. The land of Antarctica is protected from mining and oil drilling. The animals there are also protected. Still, wildlife is hurt by illegal fishing and poaching, which is illegal hunting or stealing of animals. Also, some people want to use Antarctica's rich resources. But scientists say mining and oil drilling could greatly damage the continent's plant and animal life.

Oil slicks harm ocean life

Every day, tankers criss-cross the oceans carrying huge amounts of oil. Sometimes there are accidents, and oil spills into the water. The oil spreads across the surface in huge slicks. These slicks can kill ocean life and destroy coastlines. Animals such as seabirds are coated with thick oil so they can't fly or breathe properly.

Every year, millions of gallons of oil spill into the world's oceans. Cleanup is a difficult task.

Saving the whales

People around the world are working to protect whales. Like humans, whales are mammals. They breathe air and feed milk to their young. For many years, whales were hunted freely. Great numbers were killed. Laws were finally made to protect whales. The number of whales is slowly growing, but they face threats other than hunting. Collisions with ships and the effects of pollution harm whales. But getting tangled in fishing gear is the biggest danger to whales.

A humpback whale

Risks of overfishing

Every year millions of tons of fish are caught for food. While humans need food, taking too many fish will mean trouble in the future. As schools of fish are detected with high-tech equipment, large drift nets are cast out. These nets stretch far and deep through the sea waters. They catch almost anything in their path. Overfishing means young fish are taken before they have had a chance to reproduce. Also, seals, dolphins, whales, and turtles get tangled in the nets. These animals often die before they can be freed.

Journey to the North Pole

The passengers on the icebreaker ship *Yamal* stand on the deck. So far, the journey from the port of Helsinki, Finland, has been easy sailing. But now the real adventure begins. The ship is about to make its way across the ice sheet to the North Pole.

The mighty ice-smashing machine crashes into the pack ice. Soon after, it passes Franz Josef Land. The cluster of islands has huge, jagged mountains and icebergs. There are 191 islands in all. Most of them are still unexplored.

Everyone looks out over the gleaming blue and white ice. It stretches for hundreds of miles in every direction. Some passengers are lucky enough to spot polar bears and arctic foxes. Others see seals, beluga whales, and large groups of seabirds.

A few passengers board a helicopter. They fly over the glaciers that line the coast and take photographs.

Just eight days after boarding the icebreaker, the passengers reach the North Pole. From now on, they will be able to say they stood at the top of the world!

Tomorrow, the *Yamal* will set sail for the return trip south. The memory of this cold, beautiful, faraway place will stay with the passengers forever.

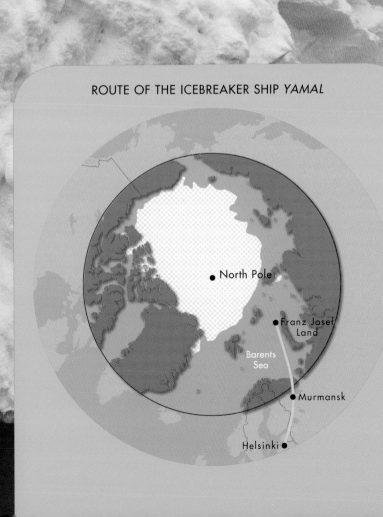

ROUTE OF THE ICEBREAKER SHIP *YAMAL*

North Pole

Franz Josef Land

Barents Sea

Murmansk

Helsinki

At-a-Glance

POLES

Antarctica

Size: 5.4 million square miles
(14 million square kilometers)

Population: no native inhabitants; research
stations are staffed by about 1,000 people in the
winter and about 4,000 people in the summer

Average temperature:
summer: 20 degrees Fahrenheit
(minus 6.7 degrees Celsius)
winter: minus 30 degrees Fahrenheit
(minus 34.4 degrees Celsius)

Highest point: Vinson Massif, 16,067 feet
(4,900 meters)

Lowest point: Bentley Subglacial Trench,
8,432 feet (2,555 m) below sea level

Common animals: elephant seal, emperor
penguin, icefish, petrel

First person to reach the South Pole:
Roald Amundsen, 1912

The Arctic

Size: 8 million square miles
(21 million square km)

Population: about 1.5 million

Average temperature:
summer: 32 degrees Fahrenheit
(0 degrees Celsius)
winter: 15 degrees Fahrenheit
(minus 9.4 degrees Celsius)

Highest point: Gunnbjornsfjeld, 12,136 feet
(3,701 m)

Lowest point: Fram Basin, 15,395 feet (4,695 m)
below sea level

Common animals: arctic hare, brown bear,
ermine, musk ox, polar bear, reindeer

First person to reach the North Pole:
Robert Edwin Peary, 1909

OCEANS

Number of oceans: 5–the Pacific Ocean, the
Atlantic Ocean, the Indian Ocean, the Arctic
Ocean, and the Southern Ocean

Largest ocean (surface area): Pacific Ocean

Smallest ocean (surface area): Arctic Ocean

Deepest ocean (average depth): Pacific Ocean

Deepest point: Mariana Trench, Pacific Ocean,
nearly 7 miles (11 km) from water's surface to the
ocean floor

Glossary

body of water – a mass of water that is in one area; such as a river, lake, or ocean

boundary – a line that shows the border of a country, state, or other land area

climate – the average weather a place has from season to season, year to year

compass rose – a symbol used to show direction on a map

continent – one of seven large land masses on Earth, including Africa, Antarctica, Asia, Australia, Europe, North America, and South America

desert – a hot or cold, very dry area that has few plants growing on it

ecosystem – all of the living and nonliving things in a certain area, including plants, animals, soil, and weather

equator – an imaginary line around Earth; it divides the northern and southern hemispheres

forest – land covered by trees and plants

glacier – a huge, slow-moving mass of ice

global warming – an increase in Earth's average temperature; it is believed to be caused by gases given off by human activity

iceberg – an ice mass that has broken away from a glacier and floats on the sea

ice cap – an ice mass that covers land and moves out from its center in all directions

ice sheet – a mass of ice that covers a very large area of land

ice shelf – an ice mass that floats on water but is still attached to an ice sheet

island – land that is completely surrounded by water

lake – a body of water that is completely surrounded by land

landform – a natural feature on Earth's surface

legend – the part of a map that explains the meaning of the map's symbols

mountain – a mass of land that rises high above the land that surrounds it

North Pole – the northern-most point on Earth

ocean – the large bodies of saltwater that cover most of Earth's surface

pack ice – floating frozen water that forms, grows, and melts in the ocean

peninsula – a body of land that is surrounded by water on three sides

plateau – a large, flat, and often rocky area of land that is higher than the surrounding land

polar – having to do with the North Pole or South Pole

population – the total number of people who live in one area

port – a place where ships can load or unload cargo (goods or people)

precipitation – water that falls from the sky in the form of rain, snow, sleet, or hail

river – a large stream of water that empties into a lake, ocean, or other river

scale – the size of a map or model compared to the actual size of things they stand for

South Pole – the southern-most point on Earth

species – groups of animals or plants that have many things in common

temperature – how hot or cold something is

tundra – land with no trees that lies in the arctic regions

valley – a low place between mountains or hills

Index

Amundsen, Roald, 15
animals, 12, 14, 15, 16, 17, 23, 24, 26, 27, 29
Antarctic Circle, 4–5, 6, 7, 10, 12, 14, 25
Antarctic Treaty, 27
Arctic Circle, 5–6, 8, 9, 10, 12, 14, 15
Arctic Ocean, 5, 8, 16, 18
Atlantic Ocean, 4, 5, 16, 22–23

Bay of Bengal, 25
black smokers, 24
blue holes, 23

climate, 6, 7, 8, 12, 15, 20–21, 24, 25
compass rose, 4

continental shelves, 18, 19
continents, 4–5, 8
currents, 20–21

doldrums, 21

ecosystems, 10, 11, 13
equator, 4–5, 21

forests, 10, 11, 12, 13
Franz Josef Land, 28

glaciers, 8, 9, 26, 29
global warming, 26

hurricanes, 21

ice, 6, 7, 8, 9
Indian Ocean, 5, 16, 25
islands, 8, 9, 19, 23

legend, 4

Mariana Trench, 18
McMurdo Station, 15
Mid-Atlantic Ridge, 22
mid-ocean ridge, 18, 22
mountains, 6, 7, 9, 18, 22

North Pole, 5, 8, 9, 28, 29

ocean ridges, 18, 19

Pacific Ocean, 4, 5, 16, 18, 24
pack ice, 9, 12
people, 14, 15
plains, 18

plants, 10, 16, 17, 23, 27
plateaus, 9
pollution, 26, 27

reefs, 23
Ross Ice Shelf, 6

salt water, 16
scale bar, 5
scientists, 14, 15, 26, 27
Scott, Robert, 15
sea trenches, 18, 19
seamounts, 18, 19
South Pole, 5, 7, 10, 15
Southern Ocean, 5, 6, 16, 24
Sundra Arc, 25
sunshine, 8

tides, 16
transportation, 15, 25
Tropic of Cancer, 4–5
Tropic of Capricorn, 4–5
tundra, 10, 11, 12, 13

valleys, 18
Vinson Massif, 6
volcanoes, 18, 19, 24, 25

Ward Hunt Ice Shelf, 9

Yamal icebreaker, 28–29

On the Web

FactHound offers a safe, fun way to find Web sites related to topics in this book. All of the sites on FactHound have been researched by our staff.

1. Visit *www.facthound.com*
2. Type in this special code: 1404838864
3. Click on the FETCH IT button.

Your trusty FactHound will fetch the best sites for you!

Look for all of the books in the Picture Window Books World Atlases series:

Atlas of Africa
Atlas of Australia
Atlas of Europe
Atlas of North America
Atlas of South America
Atlas of Southwest and Central Asia
Atlas of the Far East and Southeast Asia
Atlas of the Poles and Oceans